WINDOWS 2000 SUPPLEMENT CHAPTER
TO ACCOMPANY

OPERATING SYSTEM CONCEPTS

FIFTH EDITION

ABRAHAM SILBERSCHATZ
Bell Laboratories

PETER BAER GALVIN
Corporate Technologies

ACQUISITIONS EDITOR   Paul Crockett

MARKETING MANAGER   Katherine Hepburn

This book was set in Palatino by the author.

The paper in this book was manufactured by a mill whose forest management programs include sustained yield harvesting of its timberlands. Sustained yield harvesting principles ensure that the numbers of trees cut each year does not exceed the amount of new growth.

ISBN 0-471-41885-4

Printed in the United States of America

10 9 8 7 6 5 4 3 2 1

Chapter 25

WINDOWS 2000

The Microsoft Windows 2000 operating system is a 32-bit preemptive multitasking operating system for Intel Pentium and later microprocessors. The successor to the Windows NT operating system, it was previously named Windows NT version 5.0. Key goals for the system are portability, security, Portable Operating System Interface (POSIX) or IEEE Std. 1003.1 compliance, multiprocessor support, extensibility, international support, and compatibility with MS-DOS and MS-Windows applications. In this chapter, we discuss the key goals for this system, the layered architecture of the system that makes it so easy to use, the file system, networks and the programming interface.

25.1 ■ History

In the mid-1980s, Microsoft and IBM cooperated to develop the OS/2 operating system, which was written in assembly language for single-processor Intel 80286 systems. In 1988, Microsoft decided to make a fresh start, and to develop a "new technology" (NT) portable operating system that supported both the OS/2 and POSIX application-programming interfaces (APIs). In October 1988, Dave Cutler, the architect of the DEC VAX/VMS operating system, was hired and given the charter of building this new operating system. Originally, the team planned for NT to use the OS/2 API as its native environment, but during development, Windows NT was changed to use the 32-bit Windows API or Win32 API, reflecting the popularity of Windows 3.0. The first versions of NT were Windows NT 3.1 and Windows NT 3.1 Advanced Server. (At that time,

16-bit Windows was at Version 3.1.) Windows NT version 4.0 adopted the
Windows 95 user interface and incorporated Internet web-server and browser
software. In addition, user-interface routines and graphics code were moved
into the kernel to improve performance, with the side effect of decreased
system reliability. Although previous versions of NT had been ported to other
microprocessor architectures, Windows 2000 discontinues that practice due to
marketplace factors. Thus, *portability* now refers to portability among Intel
architecture systems. Windows 2000 uses a micro-kernel architecture (like
Mach), so enhancements can be made to one part of the operating system
without greatly affecting other parts. With the addition of Terminal Services,
Windows 2000 is a multiuser operating system.

Windows 2000 was released in 2000 and incorporated significant changes. It
adds an X.500 based directory service, better networking support, support for
Plug-and-Play devices, a new file system with support for hierarchical storage,
and a distributed file system, as well as support for more processors and more
memory.

There are four versions of Windows 2000. The Professional version is
intended for desktop use. The other three are server versions: Server, Advanced
Server, and Datacenter Server. These differ primarily in the amount of memory
and number of processors that they support. They use the same kernel and
operating-system code, but Windows 2000 Server and Advanced Server are
configured for client–server applications and can act as application servers on
NetWare and Microsoft LANs. Windows 2000 Datacenter Server now supports
up to 32 processors and up to 64 gigabytes of RAM.

In 1996, more Windows NT Server licenses were sold than all versions of
UNIX licenses. Interestingly, the code base for Windows 2000 is on the order of
30 million lines of code. Compare this size with the code base of Windows NT
version 4.0: about 18 million lines of code.

25.2 ■ Design Principles

The design goals that Microsoft has stated for Windows 2000 include extensibility, portability, reliability, compatibility, performance, and international
support.

Extensibility refers to the capacity of an operating system to keep up with
advancements in computing technology. So that changes are facilitated over
time, the developers implemented Windows 2000 using a layered architecture.
The Windows 2000 executive, which runs in kernel or protected mode, provides
the basic system services. On top of the executive, several server subsystems
operate in user mode. Among them are *environmental subsystems* that emulate
different operating systems. Thus, programs written for MS-DOS, Microsoft
Windows, and POSIX can all run on Windows 2000 in the appropriate environment. (See Section 25.4 for more information on environmental subsystems.)

Because of the modular structure, additional environmental subsystems can be added without affecting the executive. In addition, Windows 2000 uses loadable drivers in the I/O system, so new file systems, new kinds of I/O devices, and new kinds of networking can be added while the system is running. Windows 2000 uses a client–server model like the Mach operating system, and supports distributed processing by remote procedure calls (RPCs) as defined by the Open Software Foundation.

An operating system is *portable* if it can be moved from one hardware architecture to another with relatively few changes. Windows 2000 is designed to be portable. As is true of the UNIX operating system, the majority of the system is written in C and C++. All processor-dependent code is isolated in a dynamic link library (DLL), called the *hardware-abstraction layer (HAL)*. A DLL is a file that gets mapped into a process's address space such that any functions in the DLL appear as though they are part of the process. The upper layers of Windows 2000 depend on HAL, rather than on the underlying hardware, and that helps Windows 2000 to be portable. HAL manipulates hardware directly, isolating the rest of Windows 2000 from hardware differences among the platforms on which it runs.

Reliability is the ability to handle error conditions, including the ability of the operating system to protect itself and its users from defective or malicious software. Windows 2000 resists defects and attacks by using hardware protection for virtual memory, and software protection mechanisms for operating-system resources. Also, Windows 2000 comes with a native file system, the NTFS file system, that recovers automatically from many kinds of file-system errors after a system crash. Windows NT Version 4.0 has a C-2 security classification from the U.S. government, which signifies a moderate level of protection from defective software and malicious attacks. Windows 2000 is currently under evaluation by the government for that classification as well. For more information about security classifications, see Section 20.8.

Windows 2000 provides source-level *compatibility* to applications that follow the IEEE 1003.1 (POSIX) standard. Thus, they can be compiled to run on Windows 2000 without changes to the source code. In addition, Windows 2000 can run the executable binaries for many programs compiled for Intel X86 architectures running MS-DOS, 16-bit Windows, OS/2, LAN Manager, and 32-bit Windows, by using the environmental subsystems mentioned earlier. These environmental subsystems support a variety of file systems, including the MS-DOS FAT file system, the OS/2 HPFS file system, the ISO9660 CD file system, and NTFS. Windows 2000's binary compatibility, however, is not perfect. In MS-DOS, for example, applications can access hardware ports directly. For reliability and security, Windows 2000 prohibits such access.

Windows 2000 is designed to afford good *performance*. The subsystems that constitute Windows 2000 can communicate with one another efficiently by a local-procedure-call facility that provides high-performance message passing. Except for the kernel, threads in the subsystems of Windows 2000 can be preempted by higher-priority threads. Thus, the system can respond quickly to external events. In addition, Windows 2000 is designed for symmetrical multiprocessing: On a multiprocessor computer, several threads can run at the same time. The current scalability of Windows 2000 is limited, compared to that of UNIX. As of late 2000, Windows 2000 supported systems with up to 32 CPUs, whereas Solaris ran on systems with up to 64 processors. Previous versions of NT supported only up to 8 processors.

Windows 2000 is also designed for *international* use. It provides support for different locales via the national language support (NLS) API. NLS API provides specialized routines to format dates, time, and money in accordance with various national customs. String comparisons are specialized to account for varying character sets. UNICODE is Windows 2000's native character code; Windows 2000 supports ANSI characters by converting them to UNICODE characters before manipulating them (8-bit to 16-bit conversion).

25.3 ■ System Components

The architecture of Windows 2000 is a layered system of modules, as shown in Figure 25.1. The main layers are the HAL, the kernel, and the executive, all of which run in protected mode, and a large collection of subsystems that run in user mode. The user-mode subsystems are in two categories. The environmental subsystems emulate different operating systems; the *protection subsystems* provide security functions. One of the chief advantages of this type of architecture is that interactions between modules can be kept simple. The remainder of this section describes these layers and subsystems.

25.3.1 Hardware-Abstraction Layer

HAL is a layer of software that hides hardware differences from upper levels of the operating system, to help make Windows 2000 portable. HAL exports a virtual-machine interface that is used by the kernel, the executive, and the device drivers. One advantage of this approach is that only a single version of each device driver is needed—it can run on all hardware platforms without porting the driver code. HAL also provides the support for symmetric multiprocessing. For performance reasons, I/O drivers (and graphics drivers in Windows 2000) can access the hardware directly.

25.3.2 Kernel

The *kernel* of Windows 2000 provides the foundation for the executive and the subsystems. The kernel is never paged out of memory, and its execution is never preempted. It has four main responsibilities: thread scheduling, interrupt and

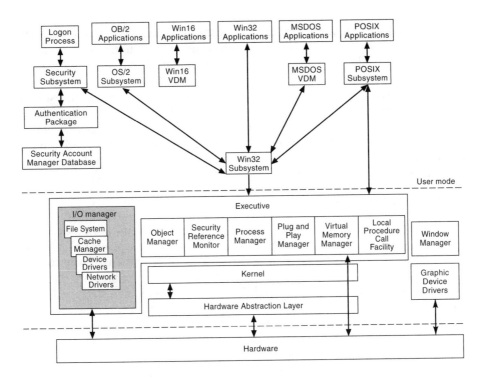

Figure 25.1   Windows 2000 block diagram.

exception handling, low-level processor synchronization, and recovery after a power failure.

The kernel is object oriented. An *object type* in Windows 2000 is a system-defined data type that has a set of attributes (data values) and a set of methods (i.e., functions or operations). An *object* is just an instance of a particular object type. The kernel performs its job by using a set of kernel objects whose attributes store the kernel data, and whose methods perform the kernel activities.

The kernel uses two sets of objects. The first set comprises the *dispatcher objects*. These control dispatching and synchronization in the system. Examples of these objects are events, mutants, mutexes, semaphores, threads, and timers. The *event object* is used to record an event occurrence and to synchronize the latter with some action. The *mutant* provides kernel-mode or user-mode mutual exclusion with the notion of ownership. The *mutex*, which is available only in kernel mode, provides deadlock-free mutual exclusion. A *semaphore object* acts as a counter or gate to control the number of threads that access some resource. The *thread object* is the entity that is run by the kernel and is associated with a *process object*. *Timer objects* are used to keep track of the time and to signal time outs when operations take too long and need to be interrupted.

The second set of kernel objects comprises the *control objects*. These objects include asynchronous procedure calls, interrupts, power notify, power status, process, and profile objects. The system uses an *asynchronous procedure call* to break into an executing thread and to call a procedure. The *interrupt object* binds an interrupt service routine to an interrupt source. The system uses the *power notify object* to call a specified routine automatically after a power failure, and the *power status object* to check whether the power has failed. A *process object* represents the virtual address space and control information necessary to execute the set of threads associated with a process. Finally, the system uses the *profile object* to measure the amount of time used by a block of code.

25.3.2.1 Threads and Scheduling

As do many modern operating systems, Windows 2000 uses the notions of processes and threads for executable code. The *process* has a virtual-memory address space, and information such as a base priority and an affinity for one or more processors. Each process has one or more *threads*, which are the units of execution dispatched by the kernel. Each thread has its own state, including a priority, processor affinity, and accounting information.

The six possible thread states are ready, standby, running, waiting, transition, and terminated. *Ready* means waiting to run. The highest-priority ready thread is moved to the *standby* state, which means that it will be the next thread to run. In a multiprocessor system, one thread is kept in the standby state for each processor. A thread is *running* when it is executing on a processor. It will run until it is preempted by a higher-priority thread, until it terminates, until its time quantum ends, or until it calls a blocking system call, such as for I/O. A thread is in the *waiting* state when it is waiting for a signal such as an I/O completion. A new thread is in the *transition* state while it is waiting for the resources necessary for execution. A thread enters the *terminated* state when it finishes execution.

The dispatcher uses a 32-level priority scheme to determine the order of thread execution. Priorities are divided into two classes: the *variable class* contains threads having priorities from 0 to 15, and the *real-time class* contains threads with priorities ranging from 16 to 31. The dispatcher uses a queue for each scheduling priority, and traverses the set of queues from highest to lowest until it finds a thread that is ready to run. If a thread has a particular processor affinity but that processor is not available, the dispatcher will skip past it, and will continue looking for a thread that is ready to run. If no ready thread is found, the dispatcher will execute a special thread called the *idle thread*.

When a thread's time quantum runs out, that thread is interrupted; if the thread is in the variable-priority class, its priority is lowered. The priority is never lowered below the base priority, however. Lowering the thread's priority tends to limit the CPU consumption of compute-bound threads. When a variable-priority thread is released from a wait operation, the dispatcher boosts the priority. The amount of the boost depends on for what the thread was waiting; for example, a thread that was waiting for keyboard I/O would get a large priority increase, whereas a thread waiting for a disk operation would get a moderate one. This strategy tends to give good response times to interactive threads that are using the mouse and windows, and enables I/O-bound threads to keep the I/O devices busy, while permitting compute-bound threads to use spare CPU cycles in the background. This strategy is used by several time-sharing operating systems, including UNIX. In addition, the current window with which the user is interacting also receives a priority boost to enhance its response time.

Scheduling can occur when a thread enters the ready or wait state, when a thread terminates, or when an application changes a thread's priority or processor affinity. If a higher-priority real-time thread becomes ready while a lower-priority thread is running, the lower-priority thread will be preempted. This preemption gives a real-time thread preferential access to the CPU when the thread needs such access. Windows 2000 is not a hard real-time operating system, however, because it does not guarantee that a real-time thread will start to execute within any particular time limit.

25.3.2.2   Exceptions and Interrupts

The kernel also provides trap handling for exceptions and interrupts that are generated by hardware or software. Windows 2000 defines several architecture-independent exceptions, including memory-access violation, integer overflow, floating-point overflow or underflow, integer divide by zero, floating-point divide by zero, illegal instruction, data misalignment, privileged instruction, page read error, guard-page violation, paging file quota exceeded, debugger breakpoint, and debugger single step.

The trap handler can handle simple exceptions; others are handled by the kernel's *exception dispatcher*. The exception dispatcher creates an exception record that contains the reason for the exception, and that finds an exception handler that can deal with the exception.

When an exception occurs in kernel mode, the exception dispatcher simply calls a routine to locate the exception handler. If no handler is found, a fatal system error occurs and the user is left with the infamous "blue screen of death" that signifies system failure.

Exception handling is more complex for user-mode processes, because an environmental subsystem (such as the POSIX system) can set up a debugger port and an exception port for every process that it creates. If a debugger port is registered, the exception handler sends the exception to that port. If the debugger port is not found or does not handle that exception, the dispatcher then attempts to find an appropriate exception handler. If a handler is not found, the debugger is called again so that it can catch the error for debugging. If a debugger is not running, a message is then sent to the process's exception port to give the environmental subsystem a chance to translate the exception. For example, the POSIX environment translates Windows 2000 exception messages into POSIX signals before sending them to the thread that caused the exception. Finally, if nothing else works, the kernel simply terminates the process that contains the thread that caused the exception.

The interrupt dispatcher in the kernel handles interrupts by calling either an interrupt service routine (such as in a device driver) or an internal kernel routine. The interrupt is represented by an interrupt object that contains all the information needed to handle the interrupt. Using an interrupt object makes it easy to associate interrupt service routines with an interrupt without having to access the interrupt hardware directly.

Various processor architectures, such as Intel or DEC Alpha, have different types and numbers of interrupts. For portability, the interrupt dispatcher maps the hardware interrupts into a standard set. The interrupts are prioritized and are serviced in priority order. There are 32 interrupt levels (IRQLs) in Windows 2000. Eight are reserved for the use of the kernel; the other 24 represent hardware interrupts via the HAL (although most x86 systems use only 16 lines). The Windows 2000 interrupts are defined in Figure 25.2.

The kernel uses an *interrupt dispatch table* to bind each interrupt level to a service routine. In a multiprocessor computer, Windows 2000 keeps a separate interrupt dispatch table for each processor, and each processor's IRQL can be set independently to mask out interrupts. All interrupts that occur at a level equal to or less than the IRQL of a processor get blocked until the IRQL is lowered by a kernel-level thread. Windows 2000 takes advantage of this property to use software interrupts to perform system functions. For instance, the kernel uses software interrupts to start a thread dispatch, to handle timers, and to support asynchronous operations.

The kernel uses the dispatch interrupt to control thread context switching. When the kernel is running, it raises the IRQL on the processor to a level above the dispatch level. When the kernel determines that a thread dispatch is required, the kernel generates a dispatch interrupt, but this interrupt is blocked

Interrupt levels	Types of interrupts
31	machine check or bus error
30	power fail
29	interprocessor notification (request another processor to act; e.g., dispatch a process or update the TLB)
28	clock (used to keep track of time)
27	profile
3–26	traditional PC IRQ hardware interrupts
2	dispatch and deferred procedure call (DPC) (kernel)
1	asynchronous procedure call (APC)
0	passive

Figure 25.2   Windows 2000 Interrupt Request Levels.

until the kernel finishes what it is doing and lowers the IRQL. At that point, the dispatch interrupt can be serviced, so the dispatcher chooses a thread to run.

When the kernel decides that some system function should be executed eventually, but not immediately, it queues a *deferred procedure call* (DPC) object that contains the address of the function to be executed, and generates a DPC interrupt. When the IRQL of the processor drops low enough, the DPC objects are executed. The IRQL of the DPC interrupt is typically higher than that of user threads, so DPCs will interrupt the execution of user threads. To avoid problems, DPCs are restricted to be fairly simple. They cannot modify a thread's memory; create, acquire or wait on objects; call system services; or generate page faults.

25.3.2.3 Low-level Processor Synchronization

The third responsibility of the kernel is to provide low-level processor synchronization. The *asynchronous procedure call* (APC) mechanism is similar to the DPC mechanism, but for more general use. The APC mechanism enables threads to set up a procedure call that will happen out of the blue at some future time. For instance, many system services accept a user-mode routine as a parameter. Instead of calling a synchronous system call that will block the thread until the system call completes, a user thread can call an asynchronous system call and supply an APC. The user thread will continue running. When the system service finishes, the user thread will be interrupted to run the APC spontaneously.

An APC can be queued on either a system thread or a user thread, although a user-mode APC will be executed only if the thread has declared itself to be *alertable*. An APC is more powerful than a DPC, in that it can acquire and wait on objects, cause page faults, and call system services. Since an APC executes in the address space of the target thread, the Windows 2000 executive uses APCs extensively for I/O processing.

Windows 2000 can run on symmetric multiprocessor machines, so the kernel must prevent two of its threads from modifying a shared data structure at the same time. The kernel uses *spin locks* that reside in global memory to achieve multiprocessor mutual exclusion. Because all activity on a processor stops when a thread is attempting to acquire a spin lock, a thread that holds a spin lock is not preempted, so it can finish and release the lock as quickly as possible.

25.3.2.4 Recovery after a Power Failure

The fourth and final responsibility of the kernel is to provide recovery after a power failure. A power-fail interrupt, which has the second-highest priority, notifies the operating system whenever a power loss is detected. The *power-notify object* provides a way for a device driver to register a routine that will be called on power restoration and ensures that devices get set to the proper state on recovery. For battery–backed-up systems, the *power status object* is useful.

Before it begins a critical operation, a driver examines the power-status object to determine whether or not the power has failed. If the driver determines that power has not failed, it raises the IRQL of its processor to powerfail, performs the operation, and resets the IRQL. This sequence of actions blocks the powerfail interrupt until after the critical operation completes.

25.3.3 Executive

The Windows 2000 executive provides a set of services that all environmental subsystems can use. The services are grouped as follows: object manager, virtual-memory manager, process manager, local-procedure-call facility, I/O manager, and security reference monitor.

25.3.3.1 Object Manager

As an object-oriented system, Windows 2000 uses objects for all its services and entities. Examples of objects are directory objects, symbolic link objects, semaphore objects, event objects, process and thread objects, port objects, and file objects. The job of the *object manager* is to supervise the use of all objects. When a thread wants to use an object, it calls the object manager's open method to get a *handle* to the object. Handles are a standardized interface to all kinds of objects. Like a file handle, an object handle is an identifier unique to a process that confers the ability to access and manipulate a system resource.

Since the object manager is the only entity that can generate an object handle, it is the natural place to check security. For instance, the object manager checks whether a process has the right to access an object when the process tries to open that object. The object manager can also enforce quotas, such as the maximum amount of memory that a process may allocate.

The object manager can keep track of which processes are using each object. Each object header contains a count of the number of processes that have handles to that object. When the counter goes to zero, the object is deleted from the name space if it is a temporary object name. Since Windows 2000 itself often uses pointers (instead of handles) to access objects, the object manager also maintains a reference count, which it increments when Windows 2000 gains access to an object and decrements when the object is no longer needed. When the reference count of a temporary object goes to zero, the object is deleted from memory. Permanent objects represent physical entities, such as disk drives, and are not deleted when the reference count and the open-handle counter go to zero.

The objects are manipulated by a standard set of methods: `create`, `open`, `close`, `delete`, `query name`, `parse`, and `security`. The final three need explanation:

- `query name` is called when a thread has a handle to an object, but wants to know the object's name.

- `parse` is used by the object manager to search for an object given the object's name.

- `security` is called when a process opens or changes the protection of an object.

The Windows 2000 executive allows any object to be given a *name*. The name space is global, so one process may create a named object, and a second process can then open a handle to the object and share it with the first process. A process opening a named object can ask for the search to be either case sensitive or case insensitive.

A name can be either permanent or temporary. A permanent name represents an entity, such as a disk drive, that remains even if no process is accessing it. A temporary name exists only while some process holds a handle to that object.

Although the name space is not directly visible across a network, the object manager's `parse` method is used to help access a named object on another system. When a process attempts to open an object that resides on a remote computer, the object manager calls the parse method, which then calls a network redirector to find the object.

Object names are structured like file path names in MS-DOS and UNIX. Directories are represented by a *directory object* that contains the names of all the objects in that directory. The object name space can grow by the addition of *object domains*, which are self-contained sets of objects. Examples of object domains are floppy disks and hard drives. It is easy to see how the name space gets extended when a floppy disk is added to the system: The floppy has its own name space that is grafted onto the existing name space.

UNIX file systems have *symbolic links*, so multiple nicknames or aliases can refer to the same file. Similarly, Windows 2000 implements a *symbolic link object*. One way that Windows 2000 uses symbolic links is to map drive names to the standard MS-DOS drive letters. The drive letters are just symbolic links that can be remapped to suit the user's preferences.

A process gets an object handle by creating an object, by opening an existing object, by receiving a duplicated handle from another process, or by inheriting a handle from a parent process, similar to the way a UNIX process gets a file descriptor. These handles are all stored in the process's *object table*. An entry in the object table contains the object's access rights and states whether the handle should be inherited by child processes. When a process terminates, Windows 2000 automatically closes all the process's open handles.

When a user is authenticated by the login process, an access-token object is attached to the user's process. The access token contains information such as the security id, group ids, privileges, primary group, and default access control list. These attributes determine which services and objects can be used by a given user.

In Windows 2000, each object is protected by an *access-control list*, which contains the security ids and access rights granted to each process. When a process attempts to access an object, the system compares the security id in the process's access token with the object's access-control list to determine whether access should be permitted. This check is done only when an object is opened, so internal Windows 2000 services that use pointers, rather than opening a handle to an object, bypass the access check.

Generally, the creator of the object determines the access-control list for that object. If none is supplied explicitly, one may be inherited from the creator object, or a default list may be obtained from the user's access-token object.

One field in the access token controls auditing of the object. Operations that are being audited get logged to the system's audit log with an identification of the user. The audit field can watch this log to discover attempts to break into the system or to access protected objects.

25.3.3.2 Virtual-Memory Manager

The virtual-memory portion of the Windows 2000 executive is the *virtual-memory (VM) manager*. The design of the VM manager assumes that the underlying hardware supports virtual-to-physical mapping, a paging mechanism, and transparent cache coherence on multiprocessor systems, and allows multiple page-table entries to map to the same page frame. The VM manager in Windows 2000 uses a page-based management scheme with a page size of 4 kilobytes. Pages of data that are assigned to a process but are not in physical memory are stored in the *paging file* on disk.

The VM manager uses 32-bit addresses, so each process has a 4 gigabytes virtual address space. The upper 2 gigabytes are identical for all processes, and are used by Windows 2000 in kernel mode. The lower 2 gigabytes are distinct for every process, and are accessible by both user- and kernel-mode threads. Note that certain configurations of Windows 2000 reserve only 1 gigabytes for operating system use, allowing a process to use 3 gigabytes of address space.

The Windows 2000 VM manager uses a two-step process to allocate memory. The first step *reserves* a portion of the process's address space. The second step *commits* the allocation by assigning space in the Windows 2000 paging file. Windows 2000 can limit the amount of paging file space that a process consumes by enforcing a quota on committed memory. A process can uncommit memory that it is no longer using to free up its paging quota. Since memory is represented by objects, when one process, the *parent*, creates a second process, the *child*, the parent can maintain the ability to access the virtual memory of the child. That is how environmental subsystems can manage the memory of their client processes. For performance, the VM manager allows a privileged process to lock selected pages in physical memory, thus ensuring that the pages will not be swapped out to the paging file.

Two processes can share memory by getting handles to the same memory object, but this approach can be inefficient since the entire memory space of an object must be committed before either process can access that object. Windows 2000 provides an alternative, called a *section object*, to represent a block of shared memory. After getting a handle to a section object, a process can map only the needed portion of the memory. This portion is called a *view*. The view mechanism also enables a process to access an object that is too large to fit into the process's paging file quota. The system can use the view to walk through the address space of the object, one piece at a time.

A process can control the use of a shared-memory section object in many ways. The maximum size of a section can be bounded. The section can be backed by disk space either in the system paging file or by a regular file (called a *memory-mapped* file). A section can be based, meaning that the section appears at the same virtual address for all processes that access it. Finally, the memory protection of pages in the section can be set to read only, read–write, execute only, guard page, or copy on write. The last two of these need some explanation. A guard page raises an exception if accessed; the exception can be used (for example) to check whether a faulty program iterates beyond the end of an array. The copy-on-write mechanism allows the VM manager to save memory. When two processes want independent copies of an object, the VM manager places only one shared copy into physical memory, but it sets the copy-on-write property on that region of memory. If one of the processes tries to modify data in a copy-on-write page, the VM manager first makes a private copy of the page for that process to use.

The virtual-address translation in Windows 2000 uses several data structures. Each process has a *page directory* that contains 1024 *page-directory entries* of size 4 bytes. Typically, the page directory is private, but it can be shared among processes if the environment so requires, Each page-directory entry points to a *page table* that contains 1024 *page-table entries* (PTEs) of size 4 bytes. Each PTE points to a 4-kilobytes *page frame* in physical memory. The total size of all the page tables for a process is 4 megabytes, so the VM manager will swap out these tables to disk when necessary. See Figure 25.3 for a diagram of this structure.

A 10-bit integer can represent all the values from 0 to 1023. Thus, a 10-bit integer can select any entry in the page directory, or in a page table. This property is used when a virtual-address pointer is translated to a byte address in physical memory. A 32-bit virtual-memory address is split into three integers, as shown in Figure 25.4. The first 10 bits of the virtual address are used as a subscript in the page directory. This address selects one page-directory entry, which points to a page table. The memory management unit (MMU) uses the next 10 bits of the virtual address to select a PTE from that page table. The PTE points to a page frame in physical memory. The remaining 12 bits of the virtual address point to a specific byte in that page frame. The MMU creates a pointer to that specific byte in physical memory by concatenating 20 bits from the PTE with the lower 12 bits from the virtual address. Thus, the 32-bit PTE has 12 bits left over; these bits describe the page. The Pentium PTE reserves 3 bits for the use of the operating system. The rest of the bits specify whether

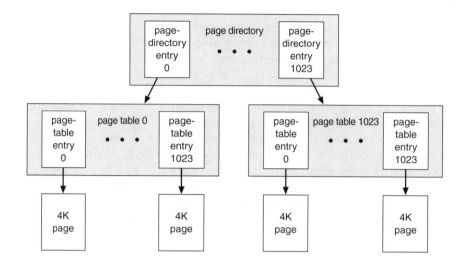

Figure 25.3   Virtual-memory layout.

the page is dirty, accessed, cacheable, read only, write through, kernel mode, or valid; thus, they describe the state of the page in memory. For more general information on paging schemes, see Section 9.4.

A page can be in one of six states: valid, free, zeroed, standby, modified, or bad. A *valid* page is in use by an active process. A *free* page is a page that is not referenced in a PTE. A *zeroed* page is a free page that has been zeroed out and is ready for immediate use. A *standby* page has been removed from the working set of a process. A *modified* page has been written to, but not yet flushed to, disk. Standby and modified pages are considered to be *transition* pages. Finally, a *bad* page is unusable because a hardware error has been detected.

The actual structure of the page-file PTE is shown in Figure 25.5. The PTE contains 5 bits for page protection, 20 bits for page-file offset, 4 bits to select the paging file, and 3 bits that describe the page state. This page-file PTE would appear as an invalid page to the hardware. Since executable code and memory-mapped files already have a copy on disk, they do not need space in a paging file. If one of these pages is not in physical memory, the PTE structure is as follows. The most significant bit is used to specify the page protection, the next

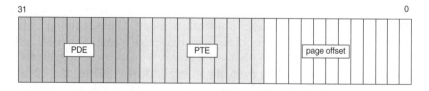

Figure 25.4   Virtual-to-physical address translation.

31   0

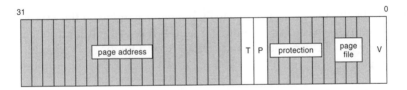

Figure 25.5   Pagefile page-table entry.

28 bits are used to index into a system data structure that indicates a file and offset within the file for the page, and the lower 3 bits specify the page state.

It is difficult to share a page between processes if every process has its own set of page tables, because each process will have its own PTE for the page frame. When a shared page is faulted in to physical memory, the physical address will have to be stored in the PTEs that belong to each process that shares the page. The protection bits and page-state bits in these PTEs will all need to be set and updated consistently. To avoid these problems, Windows 2000 uses an indirection. For every page that is shared, the process has a PTE that points to a *prototype page-table entry*, rather than to the page frame. The prototype PTE contains the page-frame address and the protection and state bits. Thus, the first access by a process to a shared page generates a page fault. After the first access, further accesses are performed in the normal manner. If the page is marked read-only, the VM manager does a copy-on-write and the process effectively does not have a shared page any longer. Shared pages never appear in the page file, but are instead found in the file system.

The VM manager keeps track of all pages of physical memory in a *page-frame database*. There is one entry for every page frame. The entry points to the PTE that points to the page frame, so the VM manager can maintain the state of the page. Page frames are linked to form (for instance) the list of zeroed pages, and the list of free pages.

When a page fault occurs, the VM manager faults in the missing page, placing that page into the first frame on the free list. But it does not stop there. Research shows that the memory referencing of a thread tends to have a property termed *locality*: When a page is used, it is likely that adjacent pages will be referenced in the near future. (Think of iterating over an array, or fetching sequential instructions that form the executable code for a thread.) Because of locality, when the VM manager faults in a page, it also faults in a few adjacent pages. This adjacent faulting tends to reduce the total number of page faults. For more information on locality, see Section 10.5.1.

If no page frames are available on the free list, Windows 2000 uses a per-process FIFO replacement policy to take pages from processes that are using more than their minimum working-set size. Windows 2000 monitors the page faulting of each process that is at its minimum working-set size, and adjusts the working-set size accordingly. In particular, when a process is started under Windows 2000, it is assigned a default working-set size of 30 pages. Windows

2000 periodically tests this size by stealing a valid page from the process. If the process continues executing without generating a page fault for the stolen page, the working set of the process is reduced by 1, and the page is added to the list of free pages.

25.3.3.3 Process Manager

The Windows 2000 process manager provides services for creating, deleting, and using threads and processes. It has no knowledge about parent–child relationships or process hierarchies; those refinements are left to the particular environmental subsystem that owns the process.

An example of process creation in the Win32 environment is as follows. When a Win32 application calls `CreateProcess`, a message is sent to the Win32 subsystem, which calls the process manager to create a process. The process manager calls the object manager to create a process object, and then returns the object handle to Win32. Win32 calls the process manager again to create a thread for the process, and finally Win32 returns handles to the new process and thread.

25.3.3.4 Local-Procedure-Call Facility

The operating system uses the *local-procedure-call* (LPC) facility to pass requests and results between client and server processes within a single machine. In particular, it uses LPC to request services from the various Windows 2000 subsystems. LPC is similar in many respects to the remote-procedure-call (RPC) mechanisms that are used by many operating systems for distributed processing across networks, but LPC is optimized for use within one Windows 2000 system.

LPC is a message-passing mechanism. The server process publishes a globally visible connection-port object. When a client wants services from a subsystem, it opens a handle to the subsystem's connection-port object, and then sends a connection request to that port. The server creates a channel and returns a handle to the client. The channel consists of a pair of private communication ports: one for client-to-server messages, and the other for server-to-client messages. Communication channels support a callback mechanism, so the client and server can accept requests when they would normally be expecting a reply.

When an LPC channel is created, one of three message-passing techniques must be specified.

1. The first technique is suitable for small messages (up to 256-byte). In this case, the port's message queue is used as intermediate storage, and the messages are copied from one process to the other.

2. The second technique is for larger messages. In this case, a shared-memory section object is created for the channel. Messages sent through the port's message queue contain a pointer and size information that refer to the

section object. Thus, the need to copy large messages is avoided: The sender places data into the shared section, and the receiver can view them directly.

3. The third technique of LPC message passing, called *quick LPC*, is used by graphical display portions of the Win32 subsystem. When a client asks for a connection that will use quick LPC, the server sets up three objects: a dedicated server thread to handle requests, a 64-kilobytes section object, and an event-pair object. An *event-pair object* is a synchronization object that is used by the Win32 subsystem to provide notification when the client thread has copied a message to the Win32 server, or vice versa. LPC messages are passed in the section object, and synchronization is performed by the event-pair object. The LPC has several advantages. The section object eliminates message copying, since it represents a region of shared memory. The event-pair object eliminates the overhead of using the port object to pass messages containing pointers and lengths. The dedicated server thread eliminates the overhead of determining which client thread is calling the server, since there is one server thread per client thread. Finally, the kernel gives scheduling preference to these dedicated server threads to improve performance. The drawback is that quick LPC uses more resources than do the other two methods, so the Win32 subsystem uses quick LPC only for the window-manager and graphics-device interfaces.

25.3.3.5 I/O Manager

The *I/O manager* is responsible for file systems, cache management, device drivers, and network drivers. It keeps track of which installable file systems are loaded, and manages buffers for I/O requests. It works with the VM manager to provide memory-mapped file I/O, and controls the Windows 2000 cache manager, which handles caching for the entire I/O system. The I/O manager supports both synchronous and asynchronous operations, provides timeouts for drivers, and has mechanisms for one driver to call another.

The I/O manager converts the requests that it receives into a standard form called an *I/O request packet* (*IRP*). It then forwards the IRP to the correct driver for processing. When the operation is finished, the I/O manager receives the IRP from the driver that most recently performed an operation, and completes the request.

In many operating systems, caching is done by the file system. Windows 2000 provides a centralized caching facility, instead. The cache manager provides cache services for all components under the control of the I/O manager, and works closely with the VM manager. The size of the cache changes dynamically, according to how much free memory is available in the system. Recall that the upper 2 gigabytes of a process's address space comprise the system area; it is identical for all processes. The VM manager allocates up to one-half of this space to the system cache. The cache manager maps files into this address space, and uses the capabilities of the VM manager to handle file I/O.

The cache is divided into blocks of 256 kilobytes. Each cache block can hold a view (i.e., a memory-mapped region) of a file. Each cache block is described by a *virtual-address control block* (*VACB*) that stores the virtual address and file offset for that view, as well as the number of processes that are using the view. The VACBs reside in a single array that is maintained by the cache manager.

For each open file, the cache manager maintains a separate VACB index array. This array has an element for each 256-kilobytes chunk of the file; so, for instance, a 2-megabytes file would have an 8-entry VACB index array. An entry in the VACB index array points to the VACB if that portion of the file is in the cache; it is null otherwise.

When a user-level read request is received by the I/O manager, the latter sends an IRP to the cache manager (unless the request specifically asks for a noncached read). The cache manager calculates which entry of that file's VACB index array corresponds to the byte offset of the request. The entry either points to the view in the cache, or is null. If it is null, the cache manager allocates a cache block (and the corresponding entry in the VACB array), and maps the view into that cache block. The cache manager then attempts to copy data from the mapped file to the caller's buffer. If the copy succeeds, the operation is completed. If the copy fails, it does so because of a page fault, which causes the VM manager to send a noncached read request to the I/O manager. The I/O manager asks the appropriate device driver to read the data, and returns the data to the VM manager, which loads the data into the cache. The data, now in the cache, are copied to the caller's buffer, and the I/O request is completed. Figure 25.6 shows an overview of all these operations. When possible, for synchronous, cached, nonlocking I/O, I/O is handled by the *Fast I/O Mechanism* This mechanism simply copies data to/from cache pages directly and utilizes the cache manager to perform any needed I/O.

A kernel-level read operation is similar, except that the data can be accessed directly from the cache, rather than being copied to a buffer in user space. To use file-system *metadata*, or data structures that describe the file system, the kernel uses the cache manager's mapping interface to read the metadata. To modify the metadata, the file system uses the cache manager's pinning interface. *Pinning* a page locks the page into a physical-memory page frame, so the VM manager cannot move or swap out the page. After updating the metadata, the file system asks the cache manager to unpin the page. Since the page has been modified, it is marked dirty, so the VM manager will flush the page to disk. Note that the metadata is actually stored in a regular file.

To improve performance, the cache manager keeps a small history of read requests, and attempts to predict future requests. If the cache manager can find a pattern in the previous three requests, such as sequential access forward or backward, it can prefetch data into the cache before the next request is submitted by the application. Then, the application may find its data already in

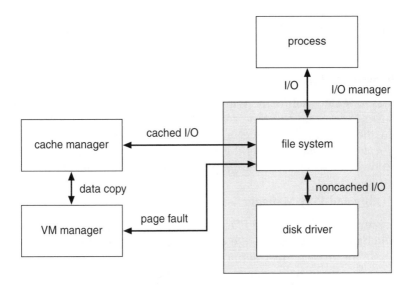

Figure 25.6   File I/O.

the cache, and may not need to wait for disk I/O. The Win32 API OpenFile and
CreateFile functions can be passed the FILE_FLAG_SEQUENTIAL_SCAN flag,
which is a hint to the cache manager to try to prefetch 192 kilobytes ahead
of the thread's requests. Typically, Windows 2000 performs I/O operations in
chunks of 64 kilobytes or 16 pages; thus, this readahead is three times the
normal amount.

The cache manager is also responsible for telling the VM manager to flush
the contents of the cache. The cache manager's default behavior is write-back
caching: it accumulates writes for 4 to 5 seconds, and then the cache-writer
thread wakes up. When write-through caching is needed, a process can set
a flag when opening the file, or the process can call an explicit cache-flush
function when needed.

A fast-writing process could potentially fill all the free cache pages before
the cache-writer thread has a chance to wake up and to flush the pages to disk.
The cache- writer prevents a process from flooding the system in the following
way: When the amount of free cache memory gets low, the cache manager
temporarily blocks processes that attempt to write data, and wakes the cache-
writer thread to flush pages to disk. If the fast-writing process is actually a
network redirector for a network file system, blocking it for too long could cause
network transfers to time out and be retransmitted. This retransmission would
waste network bandwidth. To prevent this waste, network redirectors can tell
the cache manager not to let a large backlog of writes accumulate in the cache.

Because a network file system needs to move data between a disk and
the network interface, the cache manager also provides a DMA interface to

move the data directly. Moving data directly avoids copying data through an intermediate buffer.

25.3.3.6 Security Reference Monitor

The object-oriented nature of Windows 2000 enables the use of a uniform mechanism to perform run-time access validation and audit checks for every entity in the system. Whenever a process opens a handle to an object, the *security reference monitor* checks the process's security token and the object's access-control list to see whether the process has the necessary rights.

25.3.3.7 Plug and Play Manager

The operating system uses the *Plug and Play* (*PnP*) manager to recognize and adapt to changes in the hardware configuration. For PnP to work, both the device and the driver must support the PnP standard. The PnP manager automatically recognizes installed devices and detects changes in devices as the system operates. The manager also keeps tracks of resources used by a device, as well as potential resources that could be used, and takes care of loading the appropriate drivers. This management of hardware resources (primarily interrupts and I/O memory ranges) has the goal of determining a hardware configuration in which all devices are able to operate. For example, if device B can use only interrupt 5, but device A could use 5 or 7, then the PnP manager could assign 5 to B and 7 to A. In previous versions, the user might have had to remove device A and reconfigure it to use interrupt 7, before installing device B. The user thus had to study system resources before installing new hardware, and to find out or remember which devices were using which hardware resources. The proliferation of PCCARD and USB devices also dictates that dynamic configuration of resources be supported.

The PnP manager handles this dynamic reconfiguration as follows. First, it gets a list of devices from each bus driver (for example, PCI, USB). It then loads the installed driver (or installs one, if necessary) and sends an *add-device* command to the appropriate driver for each device. The PnP manager figures out the optimal resource assignments and then sends a *start-device* command to each driver along with the resource assignment for that device. If a device needs to be reconfigured, the PnP manager sends a *query-stop* command, which asks the driver whether the device can be temporarily disabled. If the driver can disable the device, then all pending operations are completed and new operations are not allowed to be started. Next, the PnP manager sends a *stop* command; it can then reconfigure the device with another start-device command. The PnP manager also supports other commands, such as *query-remove*. This command is used when the user is getting ready to eject a PCCARD device, and which operates in a fashion similar to query-stop. The *surprise-remove* command is used when a device fails or, more likely, when a user removes a PCCARD device without using the PCCARD utility to stop it first.

The *remove* command requests that the driver stop using the device and release all resources that have been allocated to the device.

25.4 ■ Environmental Subsystems

Environmental subsystems are user-mode processes layered over the native Windows 2000 executive services to enable Windows 2000 to run programs developed for other operating systems, including 16-bit Windows, MS-DOS, POSIX, and character-based applications for 16-bit OS/2. Each environmental subsystem provides one API or application environment.

Windows 2000 uses the Win32 subsystem as the main operating environment, and thus to start all processes. When an application is executed, the Win32 subsystem calls the VM manager to load the application's executable code. The memory manager returns a status to Win32 that tells what kind of executable the code is. If it is not a native Win32 executable, the Win32 environment checks whether the appropriate environmental subsystem is running; if the subsystem is not running, it is started as a user-mode process. Then, Win32 creates a process to run the application, and passes control to the environmental subsystem.

The environmental subsystem uses the Windows 2000 LPC facility to get kernel services for the process. This approach helps Windows 2000 to be robust, because the parameters passed to a system call can be checked for correctness before the actual kernel routine is invoked. Windows 2000 prohibits applications from mixing API routines from different environments. For instance, a Win32 application cannot call a POSIX routine.

Since each subsystem is run as a separate user-mode process, a crash in one has no effect on the others. The exception is Win32, which provides all the keyboard, mouse, and graphical display capabilities. If it fails, the system is effectively disabled.

The Win32 environment categorizes applications as either graphical or character based, where a *character-based application* is one that thinks that interactive output goes to an 80 by 24 ASCII display. Win32 transforms the output of a character-based application to a graphical representation in a window. This transformation is easy: Whenever an output routine is called, the environmental subsystem calls a Win32 routine to display the text. Since the Win32 environment performs this function for all character-based windows, it can transfer screen text between windows via the clipboard. This transformation works for MS-DOS applications, as well as for POSIX command-line applications.

25.4.1 MS-DOS Environment

The MS-DOS environment does not have the complexity of the other Windows 2000 environmental subsystems. It is provided by a Win32 application called the *virtual DOS machine* (*VDM*). Since the VDM is just a user-mode process, it is paged and dispatched like any other Windows 2000 thread. The VDM has an *instruction-execution unit* to execute or emulate Intel 486 instructions. The VDM also provides routines to emulate the MS-DOS ROM BIOS and "int 21" software-interrupt services, and has virtual device drivers for the screen, keyboard, and communication ports. The VDM is based on the MS-DOS 5.0 source code; it gives the application at least 620 kilobytes of memory.

The Windows 2000 command shell is a program that creates a window that looks like an MS-DOS environment. It can run both 16-bit and 32-bit executables. When an MS-DOS application is run, the command shell starts a VDM process to execute the program.

If Windows 2000 is running on an x86 processor, MS-DOS graphical applications run in full-screen mode, and character applications can run full screen or in a window. If Windows 2000 is running on a different processor architecture, all MS-DOS applications run in windows. Some MS-DOS applications access the disk hardware directly, but they fail to run on Windows 2000 because disk access is privileged to protect the file system. In general, MS-DOS applications that directly access hardware will fail to operate under Windows 2000.

Since MS-DOS is not a multitasking environment, some applications have been written that hog the CPU—for instance, by using busy loops to cause time delays or pauses in execution. The priority mechanism in the Windows 2000 dispatcher detects such delays and automatically throttles the CPU consumption (and causes the offending application to operate incorrectly).

25.4.2 16-Bit Windows Environment

The Win16 execution environment is provided by a VDM that incorporates additional software called *Windows on Windows* that provides the Windows 3.1 kernel routines and stub routines for window manager and GDI functions. The stub routines call the appropriate Win32 subroutines, converting, or *thunking*, 16-bit addresses into 32-bit ones. Applications that rely on the internal structure of the 16-bit window manager or GDI may not work, because Windows on Windows does not really implement the 16-bit API.

Windows on Windows can multitask with other processes on Windows 2000, but it resembles Windows 3.1 in many ways. Only one Win16 application can run at a time, all applications are single threaded and reside in the same address space, and they all share the same input queue. These features imply that an application that stops receiving input will block all the other Win16 applications, just as in Windows 3.x, and one Win16 application can crash other Win16 applications by corrupting the address space. Multiple Win16 environments can coexist, however, by using the command *start /separate win16application* from the command line.

25.4.3 Win32 Environment

The main subsystem in Windows 2000 is the Win32 subsystem. It runs Win32 applications, and manages all keyboard, mouse, and screen I/O. Since it is the controlling environment, it is designed to be extremely robust. Several features of Win32 contribute to this robustness. Unlike the Win16 environment, each Win32 process has its own input queue. The window manager dispatches all input on the system to the appropriate process's input queue, so a failed process will not block input to other processes. The Windows 2000 kernel also provides preemptive multitasking, which enables the user to terminate applications that have failed or are no longer needed. Win32 also validates all objects before using them, to prevent crashes that could otherwise occur if an application tried to use an invalid or wrong handle. The Win32 subsystem verifies the type of the object to which a handle points before using that object. The reference counts kept by the object manager prevent objects from being deleted while they are still being used, and prevents their use after they have been deleted.

25.4.4 POSIX Subsystem

The *POSIX subsystem* is designed to run POSIX applications following the POSIX.1 standard, which is based on the UNIX model. POSIX applications can be started by the Win32 subsystem or by another POSIX application. POSIX applications use the POSIX subsystem server PSXSS.EXE, the POSIX dynamic link library PSXDLL.DLL, and the POSIX console session manager POSIX.EXE.

Although the POSIX standard does not specify printing, POSIX applications can use printers transparently via the Windows 2000 redirection mechanism. POSIX applications have access to any file system on the Windows 2000 system; the POSIX environment enforces UNIX-like permissions on directory trees. Several Win32 facilities are not supported by the POSIX subsystem, including memory-mapped files, networking, graphics, and dynamic data exchange.

25.4.5 OS/2 Subsystem

Although Windows 2000 was originally intended to provide a robust OS/2 operating environment, the success of Microsoft Windows led to a change; during the early development of Windows 2000, the Windows environment became the default. Consequently, Windows 2000 provides only limited facilities in the OS/2 environmental subsystem. OS/2 1.x character-based applications can run only on Windows 2000 on Intel x86 computers. Real-mode OS/2 applications can run on all platforms by using the MS-DOS environment. Bound applications, which have dual code for both MS-DOS and OS/2, run in the OS/2 environment unless the OS/2 environment is disabled.

25.4.6 Logon and Security Subsystems

Before a user can access objects on Windows 2000, that user must be authenticated by the logon subsystem. To be authenticated, a user must have an account and provide the password for that account.

The security subsystem generates access tokens to represent users on the system. It calls an *authentication package* to perform authentication using information from the logon subsystem or network server. Typically, the authentication package simply looks up the account information in a local database and checks to see that the password is correct. The security subsystem then generates the access token for the user id containing the appropriate privileges, quota limits, and group ids. Whenever the user attempts to access an object in the system, such as by opening a handle to the object, the access token is passed to the security reference monitor, which checks privileges and quotas. The default authentication package for Windows 2000 domains is Kerberos.

25.5 ■ File System

Historically, MS-DOS systems have used the *file- allocation table* (*FAT*) file system. The 16-bit FAT file system has several shortcomings, including internal fragmentation, a size limitation of 2 gigabytes, and a lack of access protection for files. The 32-bit FAT file system has solved the size and fragmentation problems, but its performance and features are still weak by comparison with modern file systems. The NTFS file system is much better. It was designed to include many features, including data recovery, security, fault tolerance, large files and file systems, multiple data streams, UNICODE names, and file compression. For compatibility, Windows 2000 provides support for the FAT and OS/2 HPFS file systems.

25.5.1 Internal Layout

The fundamental entity in NTFS is a *volume*. A volume is created by the Windows 2000 disk administrator utility, and is based on a logical disk partition. The volume may occupy a portion of a disk, may occupy an entire disk, or may span across several disks.

NTFS does not deal with individual sectors of a disk, but instead uses clusters as the unit of disk allocation. A *cluster* is a number of disk sectors that is a power of 2. The cluster size is configured when an NTFS file system is formatted. The default cluster size is the sector size for volumes up to 512 megabytes, 1 kilobytes for volumes up to 1 gigabytes, 2 kilobytes for volumes up to 2 gigabytes, and 4 kilobytes for larger volumes. This cluster size is much smaller than that for the 16-bit FAT file system, and the small size reduces the amount of internal fragmentation. As an example, consider a 1.6 gigabytes disk with 16,000 files. If you use a FAT-16 file system, 400 MB may be lost to internal fragmentation because the cluster size is 32 kilobytes. Under NTFS, only 17 megabytes would be lost when storing the same files.

NTFS uses *logical cluster numbers* (*LCNs*) as disk addresses. It assigns them by numbering clusters from the beginning of the disk to the end. Using this scheme, the system can calculate a physical disk offset (in bytes) by multiplying the LCN by the cluster size.

A file in NTFS is not a simple byte stream, as it is in MS-DOS or UNIX; rather, it is a structured object consisting of *attributes*. Each attribute of a file is an independent byte stream that can be created, deleted, read, and written. Some attributes are standard for all files, including the file name (or names, if the file has aliases), the creation time, and the security descriptor that specifies access control. Other attributes are specific to certain kinds of files. For instance, Macintosh files have two data attributes: the resource fork and the data fork. A directory has attributes that implement an index for the file names in the directory. In general, attributes may be added as necessary and are accessed using a file-name:attribute nomenclature. Most traditional data files have an *unnamed* data attribute that contains all that file's data. Note that NTFS only returns the size of the unnamed attribute in response to file-query operations, such as when running the `dir` command. Clearly, some attributes are small, and others are large.

Every file in NTFS is described by one or more records in an array stored in a special file called the *master file table* (*MFT*). The size of a record is determined when the file system is created; it ranges from 1 to 4 kilobytes. Small attributes are stored in the MFT record itself, and are called *resident* attributes. Large attributes, such as the unnamed bulk data, called *nonresident* attributes, are stored in one or more contiguous *extents* on the disk, and a pointer to each extent is stored in the MFT record. For a tiny file, even the data attribute may fit inside the MFT record. If a file has many attributes, or if it is highly fragmented and therefore many pointers are needed to point to all the fragments, one record in the MFT might not be large enough. In this case, the file is described by a record called the *base file record*, which contains pointers to overflow records that hold the additional pointers and attributes.

Each file in an NTFS volume has a unique ID called a *file reference*. The file reference is a 64-bit quantity that consists of a 48-bit file number and a 16-bit sequence number. The file number is the record number (i.e., the array slot) in the MFT that describes the file. The sequence number is incremented every time that an MFT entry is reused. This incrementation enables NTFS to perform internal consistency checks, such as catching a stale reference to a deleted file after the MFT entry has been reused for a new file.

As in MS-DOS and UNIX, the NTFS name space is organized as a hierarchy of directories. Each directory uses a data structure called a *B+ tree* to store an index of the file names in that directory. A B+ tree is used because it eliminates the cost of reorganizing the tree and has the property that the length of every path from the root of the tree to a leaf is the same. The *index root* of a directory contains the top level of the B+ tree. For a large directory, this top level contains pointers to disk extents that hold the remainder of the tree. Each entry in the directory contains the name and file reference of the file, as well as a copy of the update timestamp and file size taken from the file's resident attributes in the MFT. Copies of this information are stored in the directory, so it is efficient to generate a directory listing—all the file names, sizes, and update times are available from the directory itself, so there is no need to gather these attributes from the MFT entries for each of the files.

The NTFS volume's metadata are all stored in files. The first file is the MFT. The second file, which is used during recovery if the MFT is damaged, contains a copy of the first 16 entries of the MFT. The next few files are also special. They are called the log file, volume file, attribute-definition table, root directory, bitmap file, boot file, and bad-cluster file. The *log file*, described in Section 25.5.2, records all metadata updates to the file system. The *volume file* contains the name of the volume, the version of NTFS that formatted the volume, and a bit that tells whether the volume may have been corrupted and needs to be checked for consistency. The *attribute- definition table* indicates which attribute types are used in the volume, and what operations can be performed on each of them. The *root directory* is the top-level directory in the file-system hierarchy. The *bitmap file* indicates which clusters on a volume are allocated to files, and which are free. The *boot file* contains the startup code for Windows 2000 and must be located at a particular disk address so that it can be found easily by a simple ROM bootstrap loader. The boot file also contains the physical address of the MFT. Finally, the *bad-cluster file* keeps track of any bad areas on the volume; NTFS uses this record for error recovery.

25.5.2 Recovery

In many simple file systems, a power failure at the wrong time can damage the file-system data structures so severely that the entire volume is scrambled. Many versions of UNIX store redundant metadata on the disk, and they recover from crashes using the fsck program to check all the file-system data structures, and to restore them forcibly to a consistent state. Restoring them often involves deleting damaged files and freeing data clusters that had been written with user data but have not been properly recorded in the file system's metadata structures. This checking can be a slow process, and can lose significant numbers of data.

NTFS takes a different approach to file-system robustness. In NTFS, all file-system data-structure updates are performed inside *transactions*. Before a data structure is altered, the transaction writes a log record that contains redo and undo information; after the data structure has been changed, the transaction writes a commit record to the log to signify that the transaction succeeded. After a crash, the system can restore the file-system data structures to a consistent state by processing the log records, first redoing the operations for committed transactions, then undoing the operations for transactions that did not commit successfully before the crash. Periodically (usually every 5 seconds), a checkpoint record is written to the log. The system does not need log records prior to the checkpoint to recover from a crash. They can be discarded, so the log file does not grow without bound. The first time after system startup that an NTFS volume is accessed, NTFS automatically performs file-system recovery.

This scheme does not guarantee that all the user-file contents are correct after a crash; it ensures only that the file-system data structures (the metadata files) are undamaged and reflect some consistent state that existed prior to the crash. It would be possible to extend the transaction scheme to cover user files, but the overhead would impair the file-system performance.

The log is stored in the third metadata file at the beginning of the volume. It is created with a fixed maximum size when the file system is formatted. It has two sections: the *logging area*, which is a circular queue of log records, and the *restart area*, which holds context information, such as the position in the logging area where NTFS should start reading during a recovery. In fact, the restart area holds two copies of its information, so recovery is still possible if one copy is damaged during the crash.

The logging functionality is provided by the Windows 2000 *log-file service*. In addition to writing the log records and performing recovery actions, the log-file service keeps track of the free space in the log file. If the free space gets too low, the log-file service queues pending transactions, and NTFS halts all new I/O operations. After the in-progress operations complete, NTFS calls the cache manager to flush all data, then resets the log file and performs the queued transactions.

25.5.3   Security

The security of an NTFS volume is derived from the Windows 2000 object model. Each file object has a security-descriptor attribute stored in its MFT record. This attribute contains the access token of the owner of the file, and an access-control list that states the access privileges that are granted to each user that has access to the file.

25.5.4   Volume Management and Fault Tolerance

FtDisk is the fault-tolerant disk driver for Windows 2000. When installed, it provides several ways to combine multiple disk drives into one logical volume, so as to improve performance, capacity, or reliability.

One way to combine multiple disks is to concatenate them logically to form a large logical volume, as shown in Figure 25.7. In Windows 2000, this logical volume is called a volume set, which can consist of up to 32 physical partitions. A volume set that contains an NTFS volume can be extended without the data

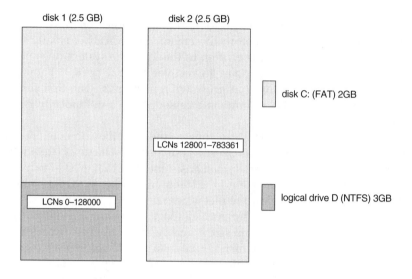

Figure 25.7   Volume set on two drives.

already stored in the file system being disturbed. The bitmap metadata on the NTFS volume are simply extended to cover the newly added space. NTFS continues to use the same LCN mechanism that it uses for a single physical disk, and the FtDisk driver supplies the mapping from a logical volume offset to the offset on one particular disk.

Another way to combine multiple physical partitions is to interleave their blocks in round-robin fashion to form what is called a stripe set, as shown in Figure 25.8. This scheme is also called *RAID level 0*, or *disk striping*. FtDisk uses a stripe size of 64 kilobytes: The first 64 kilobytes of the logical volume

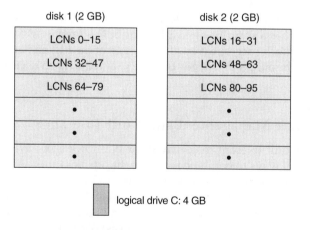

Figure 25.8   Stripe set on two drives.

are stored in the first physical partition, the second 64 kilobytes of the logical volume are stored in the second physical partition, and so on, until each partition has contributed 64 kilobytes of space. Then, the allocation wraps around to the first disk, allocating the second 64 kilobytes block. A stripe set forms one large logical volume, but the physical layout can improve the I/O bandwidth, because, for a large I/O, all the disks can transfer data in parallel.

A variation of this idea is the stripe set with parity, which is shown in Figure 25.9. This scheme is also called RAID level 5. If the stripe set has eight disks, then, for each of the seven data stripes, on seven separate disks, there will be a parity stripe on the eighth disk. The parity stripe contains the byte-wise exclusive or of the data stripes. If any one of the eight stripes is destroyed, the system can reconstruct the data by calculating the exclusive or of the remaining seven. This ability to reconstruct data makes the disk array much less likely to lose data in case of a disk failure. Notice that an update to one data stripe also requires recalculation of the parity stripe. Seven concurrent writes to seven different data stripes thus would also require seven parity stripes to be updated. If the parity stripes were all on the same disk, that disk could have seven times the I/O load of the data disks. To avoid creating this bottleneck, we spread the parity stripes over all the disks, such as by assigning them round-robin. To build a stripe set with parity, we need a minimum of three equal-sized partitions located on three separate disks.

An even more robust scheme is called *disk mirroring* or *RAID level 1*; it is depicted in Figure 25.10. A mirror set comprises two equal-sized partitions on two disks, such that their data contents are identical. When an application

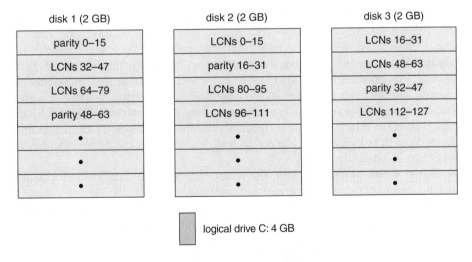

Figure 25.9   Stripe set with parity on three drives.

disk 1 (2 GB)   disk 2 (2 GB)

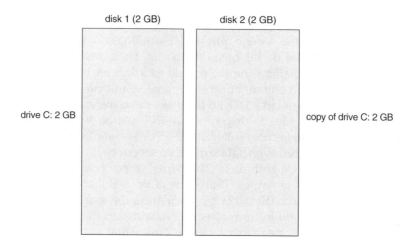

drive C: 2 GB   copy of drive C: 2 GB

Figure 25.10   Mirror set on two drives.

writes data to a mirror set, FtDisk writes the data to both partitions. If one partition fails, FtDisk has another copy safely stored on the mirror. Mirror sets can also improve the performance, because read requests can be split between the two mirrors, giving each mirror half of the workload. To protect against the failure of a disk controller, we can attach the two disks of a mirror set to two separate disk controllers. This arrangement is called a duplex set. For more information on RAID, see Section 14.5.

To deal with disk sectors that go bad, FtDisk uses a hardware technique called sector sparing, and NTFS uses a software technique called cluster remapping. Sector sparing is a hardware capability provided by many disk drives. When a disk drive is formatted, it creates a map from logical block numbers to good sectors on the disk. It also leaves extra sectors unmapped, as spares. If a sector fails, FtDisk will instruct the disk drive to substitute a spare. Cluster remapping is a software technique performed by the file system. If a disk block goes bad, NTFS will substitute a different, unallocated block by changing any affected pointers in the MFT. NTFS also makes a note that the bad block should never be allocated to any file.

When a disk block goes bad, the usual outcome is a data loss. But sector sparing or cluster remapping can be combined with fault-tolerant volumes such as stripe sets to mask the failure of a disk block. If a read fails, the system reconstructs the missing data by reading the mirror or by calculating the exclusive or parity in a stripe set with parity. The reconstructed data are stored into a new location that is obtained by sector sparing or cluster remapping.

25.5.5 Compression

NTFS can perform data compression on individual files or on all data files in a directory. To compress a file, NTFS divides the file's data into compression units, which are blocks of 16 contiguous clusters. When each compression unit is written, a data-compression algorithm is applied. If the result fits into fewer than 16 clusters, the compressed version is stored. When reading, NTFS can determine whether data have been compressed: If they have been, the length of the stored compression unit is less than 16 clusters. To improve performance when reading contiguous compression units, NTFS prefetches and decompresses ahead of the application requests.

For sparse files or files that mostly contain zeros, NTFS uses another technique to save space. Clusters that contain all zeros are not actually allocated or stored on disk. Instead, gaps are left in the sequence of virtual-cluster numbers stored in the MFT entry for the file. When reading a file, if it finds a gap in the virtual-cluster numbers, NTFS just zero-fills that portion of the caller's buffer. This technique is also used by UNIX.

25.5.6 Reparse Points

Reparse Points are a new feature in the file system that in effect return an error code when accessed. The reparse data then tell the I/O manager what to do.

Mount points are another feature added to Windows 2000; they are a form of reparse points. Unlike UNIX system, previous Windows versions provided no way to do a logical join of partitions. Each partition was assigned a drive letter that was distinct from every other partition. This meant that, among other things, that if a file system filled, the directory structure would need to be changed to add more space. Mount points would allow you to create a new volume on another drive, move the old data to the new volume, and then mount the new volume in the original place. The data would then still be usable by installed programs, since the data would appear to be in the same place as before. The mount point is implemented as a reparse point with reparse data that contains the true volume name.

The Remote Storage Services facility also uses reparse points. When a file is moved to offline storage, the original file data are replaced with a reparse point that contains information about where that file is. When the file is accessed later, the file is retrieved and the reparse point is replaced with the data from the file. For more information about hierarchical storage, see Section 14.8.1.

25.6 ■ Networking

Windows 2000 supports both peer-to-peer and client–server networking. It also has facilities for network management. The networking components in

Windows 2000 provide data transport, interprocess communication, file sharing across a network, and the ability to send print jobs to remote printers.

To describe networking in Windows 2000, we will refer to two of the internal networking interfaces, called the Network Device Interface Specification (*NDIS*) and the Transport Driver Interface (*TDI*). The NDIS interface was developed in 1989 by Microsoft and 3Com to separate network adapters from the transport protocols, so that either could be changed without affecting the other. NDIS resides at the interface between the data-link control and media-access-control layers in the OSI model and enables many protocols to operate over many different network adapters. In terms of the OSI model, the TDI is the interface between the transport layer (layer 4) and the session layer (layer 5). This interface enables any session-layer component to use any available transport mechanism. (Similar reasoning led to the streams mechanism in UNIX.) The TDI supports both connection-based and connectionless transport, and has functions to send any type of data.

25.6.1 Protocols

Windows 2000 implements transport protocols as drivers. These drivers can be loaded and unloaded from the system dynamically, although in practice the system typically has to be rebooted after a change. Windows 2000 comes with several networking protocols.

The server message-block (*SMB*) protocol was first introduced in MS-DOS 3.1. The system uses the protocol to send I/O requests over the network. The SMB protocol has four message types. The Session control messages are commands that start and end a redirector connection to a shared resource at the server. A redirector uses File messages to access files at the server. The system uses Printer messages to send data to a remote print queue and to receive back status information, and the Message message is used to communicate with another workstation.

The *Network Basic Input/Output System* (*NetBIOS*) is a hardware-abstraction interface for networks, analogous to the BIOS hardware-abstraction interface devised for PCs running MS-DOS. NetBIOS, developed in the early 1980s, has become a standard network-programming interface. NetBIOS is used to establish logical names on the network, to establish logical connections or sessions between two logical names on the network, and to support reliable data transfer for a session via either NetBIOS or SMB requests.

The *NetBIOS Extended User Interface* (*NetBEUI*) was introduced by IBM in 1985 as a simple, efficient networking protocol for up to 254 machines. It is the default protocol for Windows 95 peer networking and for Windows for Workgroups. Windows 2000 uses NetBEUI when it wants to share resources with these networks. Among the limitations of NetBEUI are that it uses the actual name of a computer as the address, and that it does not support routing.

The TCP/IP protocol suite that is used on the Internet has become the *de facto* standard networking infrastructure; it is widely supported. Windows 2000 uses TCP/IP to connect to a wide variety of operating systems and hardware platforms. The Windows 2000 TCP/IP package includes the simple network-management protocol (SNMP), dynamic host-configuration protocol (DHCP), Windows Internet name service (WINS), and NetBIOS support.

The *point-to-point tunneling protocol* (*PPTP*) is a protocol provided by Windows 2000 to communicate between remote-access server modules running on Windows 2000 Server machines and other client systems that are connected over the Internet. The remote-access servers can encrypt data sent over the connection, and they support multiprotocol virtual private networks over the Internet.

The Novell NetWare protocols (IPX datagram service on the SPX transport layer) are widely used for PC LANs. The Windows 2000 NWLink protocol connects the NetBIOS to NetWare networks. In combination with a redirector (such as Microsoft's Client Service for Netware or Novell's NetWare Client for Windows 2000), this protocol enables a Windows 2000 client to connect to a NetWare server.

Windows 2000 uses the *data-link control (DLC) protocol* to access IBM mainframes and HP printers that are connected directly to the network. This protocol is not otherwise used by Windows 2000 systems.

The *AppleTalk protocol* was designed as a low-cost connection by Apple to allow Macintosh computers to share files. Windows 2000 systems can share files and printers with Macintosh computers via AppleTalk if a Windows 2000 server on the network is running the Windows 2000 Services for Macintosh package.

25.6.2   Distributed-Processing Mechanisms

Although Windows 2000 is not a distributed operating system, it does support distributed applications. Mechanisms that support distributed processing on Windows 2000 include NetBIOS, *named pipes* and *mailslots*, windows sockets, remote procedure calls (RPC), and network dynamic data exchange (NetDDE).

In Windows 2000, NetBIOS applications can communicate over the network using NetBEUI, NWLink, or TCP/IP.

Named pipes are a connection-oriented messaging mechanism. Named pipes were originally developed as a high-level interface to NetBIOS connections over the network. A process can also use named pipes to communicate with other processes on the same machine. Since named pipes are accessed through the file-system interface, the security mechanisms used for file objects also apply to named pipes.

The name of a named pipe has a format called the uniform naming convention (*UNC*). A UNC name looks like a typical remote file name. The format of a UNC name is \\server_name\share_name\x\y\z, where the server_name identifies a server on the network; a share_name identifies any resource that is made available to network users, such as directories, files, named pipes and printers; and the \x\y\z part is a normal file path name.

Mailslots are a connectionless messaging mechanism. They are unreliable, in that a message sent to a mailslot may be lost before the intended recipient receives it. Mailslots are used for broadcast applications, such as for finding components on the network; they are also used by the Windows 2000 Computer Browser service.

Winsock is the Windows 2000 sockets API. Winsock is a session-layer interface that is largely compatible with UNIX sockets, with some Windows 2000 extensions. It provides a standardized interface to many transport protocols that may have different addressing schemes, so that any Winsock application can run on any Winsock-compliant protocol stack.

A remote procedure call (*RPC*) is a client–server mechanism that enables an application on one machine to make a procedure call to code on another machine. The client calls a local procedure—a stub routine—that packs its arguments into a message and sends them across the network to a particular server process. The client-side stub routine then blocks. Meanwhile, the server unpacks the message, calls the procedure, packs the return results into a message, and sends them back to the client stub. The client stub unblocks, receives the message, unpacks the results of the RPC, and returns them to the caller. This packing of arguments is sometimes called marshaling.

The Windows 2000 RPC mechanism follows the widely used distributed-computing environment standard for RPC messages, so programs written to use Windows 2000 RPCs are highly portable. The RPC standard is detailed. It hides many of the architectural differences between computers, such as the sizes of binary numbers and the order of bytes and bits in computer words, by specifying standard data formats for RPC messages.

Windows 2000 can send RPC messages using NetBIOS, or Winsock on TCP/IP networks, or named pipes on LAN Manager networks. The LPC facility, discussed earlier, is similar to RPC, except that in the LPC case the messages are passed between two processes running on the same computer.

It is tedious and error-prone to write the code to marshal and transmit arguments in the standard format, to unmarshal and execute the remote procedure, to marshal and send the return results, and to unmarshal and return them to the caller. Fortunately, however, much of this code can be generated automatically from a simple description of the arguments and return results.

Windows 2000 provides the Microsoft Interface Definition Language to describe the remote procedure names, arguments, and results. The compiler for this language generates header files that declare the stubs for the remote procedures, and the data types for the argument and return-value messages. It also generates source code for the stub routines used at the client side, and for an unmarshaller and dispatcher at the server side. When the application is linked, the stub routines are included. When the application executes the RPC stub, the generated code handles the rest.

DCOM (*COM*) is a mechanism for interprocess communication that was developed for Windows. COM objects provide a well defined interface to manipulate the data in the object. Windows 2000 has an extension called *DCOM* that can be used over a network utilizing the RPC mechanism to provide a transparent method of developing distributed applications.

25.6.3 Redirectors and Servers

In Windows 2000, an application can use the Windows 2000 I/O API to access files from a remote computer as though they were local, provided that the remote computer is running an MS-NET server, such as is provided by Windows 2000 or Windows for Workgroups. A redirector is the client-side object that forwards I/O requests to remote files, where they are satisfied by a server. For performance and security, the redirectors and servers run in kernel mode.

In more detail, access to a remote file occurs as follows:

- The application calls the I/O manager to request that a file be opened with a file name in the standard UNC format.

- The I/O manager builds an I/O request packet, as described in Section 25.3.3.5.

- The I/O manager recognizes that the access is for a remote file, and calls a driver called a *multiple universal-naming-convention provider* (*MUP*).

- The MUP sends the I/O request packet asynchronously to all registered redirectors.

- A redirector that can satisfy the request responds to the MUP. To avoid asking all the redirectors the same question in the future, the MUP uses a cache to remember which redirector can handle this file.

- The redirector sends the network request to the remote system.

- The remote-system network drivers receive the request and pass it to the server driver.

- The server driver hands the request to the proper local file-system driver.

- The proper device driver is called to access the data.

- The results are returned to the server driver, which sends the data back to the requesting redirector. The redirector then returns the data to the calling application via the I/O manager.

A similar process occurs for applications that use the Win32 network API, rather than the UNC services, except that a module called a multiprovider router is used, instead of a MUP.

For portability, redirectors and servers use the TDI API for network transport. The requests themselves are expressed in a higher-level protocol, which by default is the SMB protocol mentioned in Section 25.6.1. The list of redirectors is maintained in the system registry database.

25.6.4 Domains

Many networked environments have natural groups of users, such as students in a computer laboratory at school, or employees in one department in a business. Frequently, we want all the members of the group to be able to access shared resources on their various computers in the group. To manage the global access rights within such groups, Windows 2000 uses the concept of a *domain*. Previously, these domains had no relationship whatsoever to the Domain Name System that maps Internet host names to IP addresses; now, however, they are closely related. Specifically, a *Windows 2000 domain* is a group of Windows 2000 workstations and servers that shares a common security policy and user database. Since Windows 2000 now uses the Kerberos protocol for trust and authentication, a Windows 2000 domain is the same thing as a Kerberos realm. Previous versions of NT used the idea of primary and backup domain controllers; now all servers in a domain are domain controllers. In addition, previous versions required the setup of one-way trusts between domains. Windows 2000 utilizes uses a hierarchical approach based on DNS, and allows transitive trusts that can flow up and down the hierarchy. This approach reduces the number of trusts required for n domains from $n * (n - 1)$ to $O(n)$. The workstations in the domain trust the domain controller to give correct information about the access rights of each user (via the user's access token). All users retain the ability to restrict access to their own workstations, no matter what any domain controller may say.

Because a business may have many departments, and a school may have many classes, it is often necessary to manage multiple domains within a single organization. A domain tree is a contiguous DNS naming hierarchy. For example, *bell-labs.com* might be the root of the tree, with *research.bell-labs.com* and *pez.bell-labs.com* as children—(domains research and pez). A forest is a set of non-contiguous names. An example would be the trees bell-labs.com and/or lucent.com. A forest may be comprised of only one domain tree, however.

Trust relationships may be set up between domains in three ways: one-way, transitive, and cross-link. Versions of NT through version 4.0 allowed only one-way trusts to be set up. A *one-way trust* is exactly what its name implies: Domain A is told it can trust domain B. However, B would not trust A unless another relationship is configured. Under a *transitive trust*, if A trusts B and B trusts C, then A, B, and C all trust each other since transitive trusts are two-way by default. Transitive trusts are enabled by default for new domains in a tree and can only be configured among domains within a forest. The third type, a *cross-link trust*, is useful to cut down on authentication traffic. Suppose that domains A and B are leaf nodes, and that users in A often use resources in B. If a standard transitive trust is used, authentication requests must traverse up to the common ancestor of the two leaf nodes; but if A and B have a cross-linking trust established, the authentications would be sent directly to the other node.

25.6.5 Name Resolution in TCP/IP Networks

On an IP network, name resolution is the process of converting a computer name to an IP address, such as resolving www.bell-labs.com to 135.104.1.14. Windows 2000 provides several methods of name resolution, including Windows Internet Name Service (WINS), broadcast name resolution, domain name system (DNS), a hosts file, and an LMHOSTS file. Most of these methods are used by many operating systems, so we describe only WINS here.

Under WINS, two or more WINS servers maintain a dynamic database of name-to-IP address bindings, and client software to query the servers. At least two servers are used, so that the WINS service can survive a server failure, and so that the name-resolution workload can be spread over multiple machines.

WINS uses the dynamic host-configuration protocol (DHCP). DHCP updates address configurations automatically in the WINS database, without user or administrator intervention, as follows. When a DHCP client starts up, it broadcasts a discover message. Each DHCP server that receives the message replies with an offer message that contains an IP address and configuration information for the client. The client then chooses one of the configurations and sends a request message to the selected DHCP server. The DHCP server responds with the IP address and configuration information it gave previously, and with a lease for that address. The lease gives the client the right to use that IP address for a specified period of time. When the lease time is half expired, the client will attempts to renew the lease for that address. If the lease is not renewed, the client must get a new one.

25.7 ■ Programmer Interface

The Win32 API is the fundamental interface to the capabilities of Windows 2000. This section describes five main aspects of the Win32 API: access to kernel objects, sharing of objects between processes, process management, interprocess communication, and memory management.

25.7.1 Access to Kernel Objects

The Windows 2000 kernel provides many services that application programs can use. Application programs obtain these services by manipulating kernel objects. A process gains access to a kernel object named XXX by calling the CreateXXX function to open a handle to XXX. This handle is unique to that process.   Depending on which object is being opened, if the create function fails, it may return 0, or it may return a special constant named INVALID_HANDLE_VALUE. A process can close any handle by calling the CloseHandle function, and the system may delete the object if the count of processes using the object drops to 0.

Windows 2000 provides three ways to share objects between processes. The first way is for a child process to inherit a handle to the object. When the parent calls the CreateXXX function, the parent supplies a SECURITIES_ATTRIBUTES structure with the bInheritHandle field set to TRUE. This field creates an inheritable handle.   Then, the child process can be created, passing a value of TRUE to the CreateProcess function's bInheritHandle argument. Figure 25.11 shows a code sample that creates a semaphore handle that is inherited by a child process.

Assuming that the child process knows which handles are shared, the parent and child can achieve interprocess communication through the shared objects. In the example in Figure 25.11, the child process would get the value of the handle from the first command-line argument, and could then share the semaphore with the parent process.

The second way to share objects is for one process to give the object a name when that object is created, and for the second process to open that name. This method has two drawbacks. One is that Windows 2000 does not provide a way to check whether an object with the chosen name already exists. A second drawback is that the object name space is global, without regard to the object type. For instance, two applications may create an object named "pipe" when two distinct (and possibly different) objects are desired.

Named objects have the advantage that unrelated processes can share them readily. The first process would call one of the CreateXXX functions and supply a name in the lpszName parameter. The second process can get a handle to

```
...
SECURITY_ATTRIBUTES sa;
sa.nlength = sizeof(sa);
sa.lpSecurityDescriptor = NULL;
sa.bInheritHandle = TRUE;
Handle a_semaphore = CreateSemaphore(&sa,1,1,NULL);
char command_line[132] ;
ostrstream ostring(command_line,sizeof(command_line));
ostring << a_semaphore << ends;
CreateProcess("another_process.exe",command_line,NULL,NULL,TRUE, ... );
...
```

Figure 25.11   Code for a child to share an object by inheriting a handle.

```
// process A
...
Handle a_semaphore = CreateSemaphore(NULL,1,1,"MySEM1");
...
// process B
...
Handle b_semaphore = OpenSemaphore(SEMAPHORE_ALL_ACCESS,FALSE,
    "MySEM1");
...
```

Figure 25.12   Code for sharing an object by name lookup.

share this object by calling `OpenXXX` (or `CreateXXX`) with the same name, as shown in the example of Figure 25.12.

The third way to share objects is via the `DuplicateHandle` function. This method requires some other method of interprocess communication to pass the duplicated handle. Given a handle to a process, and the value of a handle within that process, a second process can get a handle to the same object, and thus share it. An example of this method is shown in Figure 25.13.

25.7.2 Process Management

In Windows 2000, a process is an executing instance of an application, and a thread is a unit of code that can be scheduled by the operating system. Thus, a process contains one or more threads. A process is started when some other process calls the `CreateProcess` routine. This routine loads any dynamic link

```
...
// process A wants to give process B access to a semaphore
// process A
Handle a_semaphore = CreateSemaphore(NULL,1,1,NULL);
// send the value of the semaphore to process B
// using a message or shared memory
...
// process B
Handle process_a = OpenProcess(PROCESS_ALL_ACCESS,FALSE,
    process_id_of_A);
Handle b_semaphore; DuplicateHandle(process_a,a_semaphore,
    GetCurrentProcess(),&b_semaphore,
    0,FALSE,DUPLICATE_SAME_ACCESS);
// use b_semaphore to access the semaphore
...
```

Figure 25.13   Code for sharing an object by passing a handle.

libraries that are used by the process, and creates a primary thread. Additional threads can be created by the CreateThread function. Each thread is created with its own stack, which defaults to one MB unless specified otherwise in an argument to CreateThread. Because some C run-time functions maintain state in static variables, such as errno, a multithread application needs to guard against unsynchronized access. The wrapper function beginthreadex provides appropriate synchronization.

Every dynamic link library or executable file that is loaded into the address space of a process is identified by an instance handle. The value of the instance handle is actually the virtual address where the file is loaded. An application can get the handle to a module in its address space by passing the name of the module to GetModuleHandle. If NULL is passed as the name, the base address of the process is returned. The lowest 64 kilobytes of the address space are not used, so a faulty program that tries to dereference a NULL pointer will get an access violation.

Priorities in the Win32 environment are based on the Windows 2000 scheduling model, but not all priority values may be chosen. Win32 uses four priority classes: IDLE_PRIORITY_CLASS (priority level 4), NORMAL_PRIORITY_CLASS (level 8), HIGH_PRIORITY_CLASS (level 13) and REALTIME_PRIORITY_CLASS (level 24). Processes are typically members of the NORMAL_PRIORITY_CLASS unless the parent of the process was of the IDLE_PRIORITY_CLASS, or another class was specified when CreateProcess was called. The priority class of a process can be changed with the SetPriorityClass function, or by an argument being passed to the START command. For example, the command START /REALTIME cbserver.exe would run the cbserver program in the REALTIME_PRIORITY_CLASS. Note that only users with the increase scheduling priority privilege can move a process into the REALTIME_PRIORITY_CLASS. Administrators and power users have this privilege by default.

When a user is running an interactive program, the system needs to provide especially good performance for that process. For this reason, Windows 2000 has a special scheduling rule for processes in the NORMAL_PRIORITY_CLASS. Windows 2000 distinguishes between the foreground process that is currently selected on the screen, and the background processes that are not currently selected. When a process moves into the foreground, Windows 2000 increases the scheduling quantum by some factor—typically by 3. (This factor can be changed via the performance option in the system section of the control panel). This increase gives the foreground process three times longer to run before a timesharing preemption occurs.

A thread starts with an initial priority determined by its class, but the priority can be altered by the SetThreadPriority function. This function takes an argument that specifies a priority relative to the base priority of its class:

- THREAD_PRIORITY_LOWEST: base − 2

- THREAD_PRIORITY_BELOW_NORMAL: base − 1

- THREAD_PRIORITY_NORMAL: base + 0

- THREAD_PRIORITY_ABOVE_NORMAL: base + 1

- THREAD_PRIORITY_HIGHEST: base + 2

Two other designations are also used to adjust the priority. Recall from Section 25.3.2 that the kernel has two priority classes: 16–31 for the real-time class, and 0–15 for the variable-priority class. THREAD_PRIORITY_IDLE sets the priority to 16 for real-time threads, and to 1 for variable-priority threads. THREAD_PRIORITY_TIME_CRITICAL sets the priority to 31 for real-time threads, and to 15 for variable-priority threads.

As we discussed in Section 25.3.2, the kernel adjusts the priority of a thread dynamically depending on whether the thread is I/O bound or CPU bound. The Win32 API provides a method to disable this adjustment, via SetProcessPriorityBoost and SetThreadPriorityBoost functions.

A thread can be created in a suspended state: The thread will not execute until another thread makes it eligible via the ResumeThread function. The SuspendThread function does the opposite. These functions set a counter, so if a thread is suspended twice, it must be resumed twice before it can run.

To synchronize the concurrent access to shared objects by threads, the kernel provides synchronization objects, such as semaphores and mutexes. In addition, synchronization of threads can be achieved by using the WaitForSingleObject or WaitForMultipleObjects functions. Another method of synchronization in the Win32 API is the *critical section*. A *critical section* is a synchronized region of code that can be executed by only one thread at a time. A thread establishes a critical section by calling InitializeCriticalSection. The application must call EnterCriticalSection before entering the critical section, and LeaveCriticalSection after exiting the critical section. These two routines guarantee that, if multiple threads attempt to enter the critical section concurrently, only one thread at a time will be permitted to proceed, and the others will wait in the EnterCriticalSection routine. The critical-section mechanism is slightly faster than the kernel-synchronization objects.

A fiber is user-mode code that gets scheduled according to a user-defined scheduling algorithm. A process may have multiple fibers in it, just as it can have multiple threads. A major difference between threads and fibers is that threads can execute concurrently, but only one fiber at a time is permitted to execute, even on multiprocessor hardware. This mechanism is included in Windows 2000 to facilitate the porting of those legacy UNIX applications that were written for a fiber-execution model.

The system creates a fiber by calling either ConvertThreadToFiber or CreateFiber. The primary difference between these functions is that CreateFiber does not begin executing the fiber that was created. To begin execution, the application must call `SwitchToFiber`. The application can terminate a fiber by calling `DeleteFiber`.

25.7.3 Interprocess Communication

One way that Win32 applications can do interprocess communication is by sharing kernel objects. Another way is by passing messages, an approach that is particularly popular for Windows GUI applications.

One thread can send a message to another thread or to a window by calling `PostMessage`, `PostThreadMessage`, `SendMessage`, `SendThreadMessage`, or `SendMessageCallback`. The difference between *posting* a message and *sending* a message is that the post routines are asynchronous: They return immediately, and the calling thread does not know when the message is actually delivered. The send routines are synchronous—they block the caller until the message has been delivered and processed.

In addition to sending a message, a thread can also send data with the a message. Since processes have separate address spaces, the data must be copied. The system copies them by calling `SendMessage` to send a message of type `WM_COPYDATA` with a `COPYDATASTRUCT` data structure that contains the length and address of the data to be transferred. When the message is sent, Windows 2000 copies the data to a new block of memory and gives the virtual address of the new block to the receiving process.

Unlike the 16-bit windows environment, every Win32 thread has its own input queue from which the thread receives messages. (All input is received via messages.) This structure is more reliable than the shared input queue of 16-bit windows, because, with separate queues, one stuck application cannot block input to the other applications. If a Win32 application does not call `GetMessage` to handle events on its input queue, the queue will fill up, and after about 5 seconds the system will mark the application as "Not Responding."

25.7.4 Memory Management

The Win32 API provides several ways for an application to use memory: virtual memory, memory-mapped files, heaps, and thread-local storage.

An application calls `VirtualAlloc` to reserve or commit virtual memory, and `VirtualFree` to decommit or release the memory. These functions enable the application to specify the virtual address at which the memory is allocated. They operate on multiples of the memory pagesize, and the starting address of an allocated region must be greater than 0×10000. Examples of these functions appear in Figure 25.14.

A process may lock some of its committed pages into physical memory by calling `VirtualLock`. The maximum number of pages that a process can lock is 30, unless the process first calls `SetProcessWorkingSetSize` to increase the minimum working-set size.

```
...
// allocate 16 MB at the top of our address space
void *buf = VirtualAlloc(0,0×1000000,MEM_RESERVE |  MEM_TOP_DOWN,
    PAGE_READWRITE);
// commit the upper 8 MB of the allocated space
VirtualAlloc(buf + 0×800000,0×800000,MEM_COMMIT,PAGE_READWRITE);
// do some stuff with it
// decommit
VirtualFree(buf + 0×800000,0×800000,MEM_DECOMMIT);
// release all the allocated address space
VirtualFree(buf,0,MEM_RELEASE);
...
```

Figure 25.14 Code fragments for allocating virtual memory.

Another way for an application to use memory is by memory mapping a file into its address space. Memory mapping is also a convenient way for two processes to share memory: Both processes map the same file into their virtual memory. Memory mapping is a multistage process, as you can see in the example of Figure 25.15.

If a process wants to map some address space just to share a memory region with another process, no file is needed. The process can call Create-FileMapping with a file handle of 0xffffffff and a particular size. The resulting file-mapping object can be shared by inheritance, by name lookup, or by duplication.

```
...
// open the file or create it if it does not exist
HANDLE hfile = CreateFile("somefile",GENERIC_READ | GENERIC_WRITE,
    FILE_SHARE_READ | FILE_SHARE_WRITE,NULL,OPEN_ALWAYS,
    FILE_ATTRIBUTE_NORMAL,
    NULL);
// create the file mapping 8 MB in size
HANDLE hmap = CreateFileMapping(hfile,PAGE_READWRITE,
    SEC_COMMIT,0,0×800000,"SHM_1");
// get a view to the space mapped
void *buf = MapViewOfFile(hmap,FILE_MAP_ALL_ACCESS,0,0,0×800000);
// do some stuff with it
// unmap the file
UnmapViewOfFile(buf);
CloseHandle(hmap);
CloseHandle(hfile); ...
```

Figure 25.15 Code fragments for memory mapping of a file.

```
// reserve a slot for a variable
DWORD var_index = TlsAlloc();
// set it to some value
TlsSetValue(var_index,10);
// get the value back
int var = TlsGetValue(var_index);
// release the index
TlsFree(var_index);
```

Figure 25.16   Code for dynamic thread-local storage.

The third way for applications to use memory is a heap. A heap in the Win32 environment is just a region of reserved address space. When a Win32 process is initialized, it is created with a 1-MB default heap. Since many Win32 functions use the default heap, access to the heap is synchronized to protect the heap's space-allocation data structures from being damaged by concurrent updates by multiple threads. Win32 provides several heap-management functions so that a process can allocate and manage a private heap. These functions are HeapCreate, HeapAlloc, HeapRealloc, HeapSize, HeapFree, and HeapDestroy. The Win32 API also provides the HeapLock and HeapUnlock functions to enable a thread to gain exclusive access to a heap. Unlike VirtualLock, these functions perform only synchronization; they do not lock pages into physical memory

The fourth way for applications to use memory is a thread-local storage mechanism. Functions that rely on global or static data typically fail to work properly in a multithreaded environment. For instance, the C run-time function strtok uses a static variable to keep track of its current position while parsing a string. For two concurrent threads to execute strtok correctly, they need separate "current position" variables. The *thread-local* storage mechanism allocates global storage on a per-thread basis. It provides both dynamic and static methods of creating thread-local storage. The dynamic method is illustrated by the example in Figure 25.16.

To use a thread-local static variable, the application would declare the variable as follows to ensure that every thread has its own private copy:

```
__declspec(thread) DWORD cur_pos = 0;
```

25.8 ■ Summary

Microsoft designed Windows 2000 to be an extensible, portable operating system—one able to take advantage of new techniques and hardware. Windows 2000 supports multiple operating environments and symmetric multiprocessing. The use of kernel objects to provide basic services, and the support for client–server computing, enable Windows 2000 to support a wide variety of application environments. For instance, Windows 2000 can run programs compiled for MS-DOS, Win16, Windows 95, Windows 2000, and/or POSIX. It provides virtual memory, integrated caching, and preemptive scheduling. Windows 2000 supports a security model stronger than those of previous Microsoft operating systems, and includes internationalization features. Windows 2000 runs on a wide variety of computers, so users can choose and upgrade hardware to match their budgets and performance requirements, without needing to alter the applications that they run.

■ Exercises

25.1 What are some reasons why moving the graphics code in Windows NT from user mode to kernel mode might decrease the reliability of the system? Which of the original design goals for Windows NT does this degradation violate?

25.2 The Windows 2000 VM manager uses a two-stage process to allocate memory. Identify several ways in which this approach is beneficial?

25.3 Discuss some advantages and some disadvantages of the particular page-table structure used in Windows 2000.

25.4 What is the maximum number of page faults that could occur in the access of (a) a virtual address, and of (b) a shared virtual address? What hardware mechanism is provided by most processors to decrease these numbers?

25.5 What is the purpose of a prototype page-table entry in Windows 2000?

25.6 What are the steps the cache manager must take to copy data into and out of the cache?

25.7 What are the main problems involved in running 16-bit Windows applications in a VDM? Identify the solutions chosen by Windows 2000 for each of these problems. For each solution, name at least one drawback.

25.8 What changes would be needed for Windows 2000 to run a process that uses a 64-bit address space?

25.9 Windows 2000 has a centralized cache manager. What are the advantages and disadvantages of this cache manager?

25.10 Windows 2000 uses a packet-driven I/O system. Discuss the pros and cons of the packet-driven approach to I/O.

25.11 Consider a main-memory database of 1 terabytes. What mechanisms in Windows 2000 could you use to access this database?

Bibliographical Notes

Solomon and Russinovich [2000] gives an overview of Windows 2000 and considerable technical detail about the system internals and components. Tate [2000] is a good reference on using Windows 2000. The Microsoft Windows 2000 Server Resource Kit (Microsoft [2000b]) is a six-volume set helpful for using and deploying Windows 2000. The Microsoft Developer Network Library (Microsoft [2000a]) is issued quarterly. It provides a wealth of information on Windows 2000 and other Microsoft products. Iseminger [2000] provides a good reference on the Windows 2000 Active Directory. Richter [1997] gives a detailed discussion on writing programs that use the Win32 API. Silberschatz et al. [1997] contains a good discussion of B+ trees.